PENGUIN BOOKS

Poems and Readings for Births and C

Julia Watson was born in Wales, and read English and Drama at Exeter University. She is the editor of two previous anthologies: *Poems and Readings for Weddings* and *Poems and Readings for Funerals*.

Her many television appearances include several series of *Casualty* for the BBC playing Dr Baz, and Thames TV's long-running comedy series *Never the Twain* with Donald Sinden and Windsor Davies. She has worked extensively in theatre, and has appeared in *Danton's Death*, *Major Barbara*, *She Stoops to Conquer* and *Wild Honey* for the National Theatre.

In 2003 she received a Grammy nomination (Best Performance) for *The Woman and the Hare* with the Nashe Ensemble.

Julia Watson is married to the poet David Harsent. They live with their daughter in Barnes, south-west London.

Poems and Readings
for Births and Christenings

EDITED BY JULIA WATSON

PENGUIN BOOKS

PENGUIN BOOKS

Published by the Penguin Group
Penguin Books Ltd, 80 Strand, London WC2R ORL, England
Penguin Group (USA) Inc., 375 Hudson Street, New York, New York 10014, USA
Penguin Group (Canada), 90 Eglinton Avenue East, Suite 700, Toronto, Ontario, Canada M4P 2Y3
(a division of Pearson Penguin Canada Inc.)
Penguin Ireland, 25 St Stephen's Green, Dublin 2, Ireland
(a division of Penguin Books Ltd)
Penguin Group (Australia), 250 Camberwell Road,
Camberwell, Victoria 3124, Australia (a division of Pearson Australia Group Pty Ltd)
Penguin Books India Pvt Ltd, 11 Community Centre,
Panchsheel Park, New Delhi – 110 017, India
Penguin Group (NZ), cnr Airborne and Rosedale Roads, Albany,
Auckland 1310, New Zealand (a division of Pearson New Zealand Ltd)
Penguin Books (South Africa) (Pty) Ltd, 24 Sturdee Avenue,
Rosebank 2196, South Africa

Penguin Books Ltd, Registered Offices: 80 Strand, London WC2R ORL, England

www.penguin.com

Published in Penguin Books 2005
1

This collection copyright © Julia Watson, 2005
The acknowledgements on pp. 141–3 constitute an extension of this copyright page

Set in 11/13 pt Monotype Garamond
Typeset by Rowland Phototypesetting Ltd, Bury St Edmunds, Suffolk
Printed in England by Clays Ltd, St Ives plc

My thanks to
Liz Beaumont
whose suggestion gave rise
to this book

Contents

Where am I going? . . .

The joys of motherhood . . .

The joys of fatherhood . . .

The finest baby in the world . . .

If you can keep your head when all about you . . .

Foreword

As an actress married to a poet, I am quite often asked to suggest a poem or a reading for a particular event, and so I had the idea for a series of anthologies with poems and readings for different secular and religious ceremonies. This one is to help welcome a baby into the family, whether at a traditional religious service, at a naming ceremony in a register office or at a gathering of family and friends at home.

In every culture across history man has celebrated the three great milestones in life – birth, marriage and death – with an event, a ceremony.

Traditionally the birth of a child has been marked by some form of religious 'welcoming' service, and, while many people still prefer this option, there has been, in an increasingly secular society, a decline in the numbers of people involved with organized religion. This has meant that fewer people have a religious marriage ceremony and consequently are less likely to mark their child's birth with a ritual linked to their particular faith.

However, in my experience, parents are still keen to ask friends to become 'godparents' to their children, even without a formal christening service, because they recognize the value of that unique relationship.

In response to a wish by many parents to celebrate the birth of their offspring with some formal occasion, local authorities in the UK are adopting a scheme similar to one that has been available in America for some time and offering a civil *naming* ceremony, in the same way that they offer a civil marriage ceremony. This scheme was first introduced in 2002 and has been growing in popularity. Although the certificate issued with the register office ceremony has no validity in law and in no way replaces the birth certificate, it is part of the baby's and family's personal histories.

Because the idea of a naming ceremony is a relatively new one, I have included a blueprint for how it might be conducted. Do feel free to adapt it to your own taste.

Julia Watson

Anonymous

What are little boys made of, made of?
What are little boys made of?
　Frogs and snails
　And puppy-dogs' tails,
That's what little boys are made of.

What are little girls made of, made of?
What are little girls made of?
　Sugar and spice
　And all things nice,
That's what little girls are made of.

Where did you come from, baby dear? . . .

They might not need me – yet they might –
I'll let my heart be just in sight –
A smile so small as mine might be
Precisely their necessity.

Emily Dickinson (1830–86)

The Baby

Where did you come from, baby dear?
Out of the everywhere into the here.

Where did you get your eyes so blue?
Out of the sky as I came through.

What makes the light in them sparkle and spin?
Some of the starry spikes left in.

Where did you get that little tear?
I found it waiting when I got here.

What makes your forehead so smooth and high?
A soft hand stroked it as I went by.

What makes your cheek like a warm white rose?
Something better than any one knows.

Whence that three-cornered smile of bliss?
Three angels gave me at once a kiss.

Where did you get that pearly ear?
God spoke, and it came out to hear.

Where did you get those arms and hands?
Love made itself into hooks and bands.

Feet, whence did you come, you darling things?
From the same box as the cherubs' wings.

How did they all just come to be you?
God thought about me, and so I grew.

But how did you come to us, you dear?
God thought of you, and so I am here.

George *MacDonald* (1824–1905)

I Know a Baby

I know a baby, such a baby –
Round blue eyes and cheeks of pink,
Such an elbow furrowed with dimples,
Such a wrist where creases sink.

'Cuddle and love me, cuddle and love me,'
Crows the mouth of coral pink:
Oh the bald head, and oh the sweet lips,
And oh the sleepy eyes that wink!

Christina Rossetti (1830–94)

Infant Joy

'I have no name:
I am but two days old.'
What shall I call thee?
'I happy am,
Joy is my name.'
Sweet joy befall thee!

Pretty joy!
Sweet joy, but two days old.
Sweet Joy I call thee:
Thou dost smile,
I sing the while,
Sweet joy befall thee!

from *Songs of Innocence*,
William Blake (1757–1827)

'There is song in man'

There is song in man
There is song in woman
And there is the child's song.
When that song comes
There will be no words.
Do not ask where they are.
Just listen to the song.
Listen to it –
Learn it –
It is the greatest song of all.

Spike Milligan (1918–2002)

'Little girl, be careful what you say'

Little girl, be careful what you say
when you make talk with words, words –
for words are made of syllables
and syllables, child, are made of air –
and air is so thin – air is the breath of God –
air is finer than fire or mist,
finer than water or moonlight,
finer than spiderwebs in the moon,
finer than water-flowers in the morning:
   and words are strong, too,
    stronger than rocks or steel
stronger than potatoes, corn, fish, cattle,
and soft, too, soft as little pigeon-eggs,
soft as the music of humming bird wings.
   So, little girl, when you speak greetings,
when you tell jokes, make wishes or prayers,
   be careful, be careless, be careful,
   be what you wish to be.

Carl Sandburg (1878–1967)

Invocation

Blessing, sleep and grow taller in sleeping.
Lie ever in kind keeping.
Infants curl in a cowrie of peace
And should lie lazy. After this ease,
When the soul out of its safe shell goes,
Stretched as you stretch those knees and toes,
What should I wish you? Intelligence first,
In a credulous age by instruction cursed.
Take from us both what immunity
We have from the germ of the printed lie.
Your father's calm temper I wish you, and
The shaping power of his confident hand.
Much, too, that is different and your own;
And may we learn to leave you alone.
For your part, forgive us the pain of living,
Grow in that harsh sun great-hearted and loving.
Sleep, little honey, then; sleep while the powers
Of the Nine Bright Shiners and the Seven Stars
Harmless, encircle: the natural world
Lifegiving, neutral, unless despoiled
By our greed or scorn. And wherever you sleep –
My arms outgrown – or waking weep,
Life is your lot: you lie in God's hand,
In his terrible mercy, world without end.

from 'For a Christening',
Anne Ridler (1912–2001)

Étude Réaliste

A baby's feet, like sea-shells pink,
   Might tempt, should Heaven see meet,
An angel's lips to kiss, we think,
      A baby's feet.

Like rose-hued sea-flowers toward the heat
   They stretch and spread and wink
Their ten soft buds that part and meet.

No flower-bells that expand and shrink
   Gleam half so heavenly sweet
As shine on life's untrodden brink
      A baby's feet.

A baby's hands, like rosebuds furled,
   Whence yet no leaf expands,
Ope if you touch, though close upcurled,
   A baby's hands.

Then, even as warriors grip their brands
   When battle's bolt is hurled,
They close, clenched hard like tightening bands.

No rosebuds yet by dawn impearled
   Match, even in loveliest lands,
   The sweetest flowers in all the world –
      A baby's hands.

iii

A baby's eyes, ere speech begin,
   Ere lips learn words or sighs,
Bless all things bright enough to win
    A baby's eyes.

Love, while the sweet thing laughs and lies,
   And sleep flows out and in,
Lies perfect in them Paradise.

Their glance might cast out pain and sin,
   Their speech make dumb the wise.
By mute glad godhead felt within
    A baby's eyes.

Algernon Charles Swinburne (1837–1909)

'Dear Babe, that sleepest cradled by my side'

Dear Babe, that sleepest cradled by my side,
Whose gentle breathings, heard in this deep calm,
Fill up the interspersed vacancies
And momentary pauses of the thought!
My babe so beautiful! it thrills my heart
With tender gladness, thus to look at thee,
And think that thou shalt learn far other lore,
And in far other scenes! For I was reared
In the great city, pent 'mid cloisters dim,
And saw nought lovely but the sky and stars.
But *thou*, my babe! shalt wander like a breeze
By lakes and sandy shores . . .

Therefore all seasons shall be sweet to thee,
Whether the summer clothe the general earth
With greenness, or the redbreast sit and sing
Betwixt the tufts of snow on the bare branch
Of mossy apple-tree, while the night thatch
Smokes in the sun-thaw; whether the eave-drops fall
Heard only in the trances of the blast,
Or if the secret ministry of frost
Shall hang them up in silent icicles,
Quietly shining to the quiet Moon.

from 'Frost at Midnight',
Samuel Taylor Coleridge (1772–1834)

You're

Clownlike, happiest on your hands,
Feet to the stars, and moon-skulled,
Gilled like a fish. A common-sense
Thumbs-down on the dodo's mode.
Wrapped up in yourself like a spool,
Trawling your dark as owls do.
Mute as a turnip from the Fourth
Of July to All Fools' Day,
O high-riser, my little loaf.

Vague as fog and looked for like mail,
Farther off than Australia.
Bent-backed Atlas, our travelled prawn.
Snug as a bud and at home
Like a sprat in a pickle jug
A creel of eels, all ripples,
Jumpy as a Mexican bean.
Right, like a well-done sum.
A clean slate, with your own face on.

Sylvia Plath (1932–63)

Child of My Heart

Child heart,
  Wild heart!
What can I bring you
What can I sing you,
You who have come from a glory afar,
Called into Time from a secret star?

Fleet one,
  Sweet one!
Whose was the wild hand
Shaped you in child-land,
Pouring the soul as a fearful fire,
Sending you forth at a dream's desire?

Strong child,
  Song child!
Who can unravel
All your long travel
Out of the Mystery, birth after birth –
Out of the dim worlds deeper than Earth?

Mad thing,
  Glad thing!
How will Life tame you?
How will God name you?
All that I know is that you are to me
Wind over water, star on the sea.

Dear heart,
  Near heart!
Long is the journey,
Hard is the tourney:
Would I could be by your side if you fall –
Would that my own heart could suffer it all!

Edwin Markham (1852–1940)

'Hush, little baby, don't say a word'

Hush, little baby, don't say a word,
Mama's gonna buy you a mockingbird.

If that mockingbird don't sing,
Mama's gonna buy you a diamond ring.

If that diamond ring is brass,
Mama's gonna buy you a looking glass.

If that looking glass gets broke,
Mama's gonna buy you a billy-goat.

If that billy-goat won't pull,
Mama's gonna buy you a cart and bull.

If that card and bull turns over,
Mama's gonna buy you a dog named Rover.

If that dog named Rover won't bark,
Mama's gonna buy you a horse and cart.

If that horse and cart falls down,
You'll still be the sweetest little baby in town.

Traditional

Children

Whether by careless accident
or careful plan
we are where they begin.

They grow in us
like germs or fictions
and we grow big with them.

Red, mewling strangers
they tear our thresholds
and immediately we love them.

When people say
they look like us
we smile and blush.

We listen for their cries
as if we felt their pain
and hunger deep in us

and hold them tightly
in our arms as if we'd found
a lost part of ourselves.

We want to give them
all the things we never had,
to make it up to them

for all the times
when we were hurt or sad,
to start again and put right

our mistakes in them,
to run in front of them
with warning flags.

We who've failed to be
the authors of our lives
write theirs.

We make them heroes,
stars whose happy endings
will scatter light in ours.

We feed them with our dreams
then wait and watch
like gardeners for flowers.

Vicki Feaver (1943–)

Response

For Eileen

Sleep, little one, sleep for me,
Sleep the deep sleep of love.
You are loved, awake or dreaming,
You are loved.

Dancing winds will sing for you,
Ancient gods will pray for you,
A poor lost poet will love you,
As stars appear
In the dark
Skies.

Bob Kaufman (1925–86)

For My Son

You come from poets, kings, bankrupts, preachers,
    attempted bankrupts, builders of cities, salesmen,
the great rabbis, the kings of Ireland, failed drygoods
    storekeepers, beautiful women of the songs,
great horsemen, tyrannical fathers at the shore of ocean,
    the western mothers looking west beyond from their
    windows,
the families escaping over the sea hurriedly and by night –
the roundtowers of the Celtic violet sunset,
the diseased, the radiant, fliers, men thrown out of town,
    the man bribed by his cousins to stay out of town,
    teachers, the cantor on Friday evening, the lurid newspapers,
strong women gracefully holding relationship, the Jewish
    girl going to parochial school, the boys racing their iceboats
    on the Lakes,
the woman still before the diamond in the velvet window,
    saying 'Wonder of nature.'

Like all men,
you come from singers, the ghettos, the famines, wars and
    refusal of wars, men who built villages
that grew to our solar cities, students, revolutionists, the
    pouring of buildings, the market newspapers,
a poor tailor in a darkening room,
a wilderness man, the hero of mines, the astronomer, a
    white-faced woman hour on hour teaching piano and her
    crippled wrist,
like all men,
you have not see your father's face
but he is known to you forever in song, the coast of the
skies, in dream, wherever you find man playing his
    part as father, father among our light, among our darkness,

and in your self made whole, whole with yourself and
   whole with others,
the stars your ancestors.

Muriel Rukeyser (1913–80)

A Cradle Song

The angels are stooping
Above your bed;
They weary of trooping
With the whimpering dead.

God's laughing in Heaven
To see you so good;
The Sailing Seven
Are gay with His mood.

I sigh that kiss you,
For I must own
That I shall miss you
When you have grown.

W. B. Yeats (1865–1939)

Laus Infantium

In praise of little children I will say
God first made man, then found a better way
For woman, but his third way was the best.
Of all created things, the loveliest
And most divine are children. Nothing here
Can be to us more gracious or more dear.
And though, when God saw all his works were good,
There was no rosy flower of babyhood,
'Twas said of children in a later day
That none could enter Heaven save such as they.

The earth, which feels the flowering of a thorn,
Was glad, O little child, when you were born;
The earth, which thrills when skylarks scale the blue,
Soared up itself to God's own Heaven in you;

And Heaven, which loves to lean down and to glass
Its beauty in each dewdrop on the grass –
Heaven laughed to find your face so pure and fair,
And left, O little child, its reflex there.

William Canton (1845–1926)

A Cradle Song

Sweet dreams, form a shade
O'er my lovely infant's head;
Sweet dreams of pleasant streams
By happy, silent, moony beams.

Sweet Sleep, with soft down
Weave thy brows an infant crown.
Sweet Sleep, angel mild,
Hover o'er my happy child.

Sweet smiles, in the night
Hover over my delight;
Sweet smiles, mother's smiles,
All the livelong night beguiles.

Sweet moans, dovelike sighs,
Chase not slumber from thy eyes.
Sweet moans, sweeter smiles,
All the dovelike moans beguiles.

Sleep, sleep, happy child,
All creation slept and smil'd;
Sleep, sleep, happy sleep,
While o'er thee thy mother weep.

Sweet babe, in thy face
Holy image I can trace.
Sweet babe, once like thee,
Thy Maker lay, and wept for me,

Wept for me, for thee, for all,
When He was an infant small.
Thou His image ever see,
Heavenly face that smiles on thee,

Smiles on thee, on me, on all;
Who became an infant small.
Infant smiles are His own smiles;
Heaven and earth to peace beguiles.

from *Songs of Innocence*,
William Blake (1757–1827)

Pledge

Here in my cradling arms
Safe from any harm
Let the loved-one lie.

There's room for you in my heart
And room for you in my house
Until the day I die.

Dora Mann (1943–)

Heavy as Lead

i

For our children are the children of our flesh
And the body of our love. The love that was
Before child-birth seems airy, feathery,
Frond-like now, a spirit moving grass.

Lovers' love which is a spirit must take
Flesh, the bodies we beget and bear;
And flesh is heavy and opaque
And a lodestone to care.

ii

Heavy as lead, heavy as water
That seeks with obdurate art
And finds for resting-place the deepest part,
So heavy in us is our tender daughter.

Heavy in us – to God or stranger
A spirit or leaf-light sapling,
To us she is a leaden anchor grappling
To sand and central rock; the ocean-ranger

Strains against it. Heavy as earth
On a tree's roots when the green tree,
Its sunward frame, is racing like a sea.
So heavy is child-love, and holds us as if she,
Our child, were ground that gave us birth.

E. J. Scovell (1907–99)

The Twins

Not because of their beauty – though they are slender
as saplings of white cedar, and long as lilies –
not because of their delicate dancing step,
or their brown hair sideways blown like the manes of fillies –
it is not for their beauty that the crowd in the street
wavers like dry leaves around them on the wind.
It is the chord, the intricate unison
of one and one, strikes home to the watcher's mind.

How sweet is the double gesture, the mirror-answer;
same hand woven in same, like arm in arm.
Salt blood like tears freshens the crowd's dry veins,
and moving in its web of time and harm
the unloved heart asks, 'Where is my reply,
my kin, my answer? I am driven and alone.'
Their serene eyes seek nothing. They walk by.
They move into the future and are gone.

Judith Wright (1915–2000)

'All the kind gods' grace'

All the kind gods' grace,
All their love, embrace
Ever either face,
  Ever brood above them:
All soft wings of hours
Screen them as with flowers
From all beams and showers:
  All life's seasons love them.

When the dews of sleep
Falling lightliest keep
Eyes too close to peep
  Forth and laugh off rest.
Joy from face to feet
Fill them, as is meet:
Life to them be sweet
  As their mother's breast.

When those dews are dry,
And in day's bright eye
Looking full they lie
  Bright as rose and pearl,
All returns of joy
Pure of time's alloy
Bless the rose-red boy,
  Guard the rose-white girl

from 'Twins',
Algernon Charles Swinburne
(1837–1909)

Welcome

Welcome to sunlight
Welcome to the soft rain on your face

Welcome to the rush of the wind
Welcome to the hush of the sea

Welcome to much joy and a little sorrow
Welcome to birdsong

Welcome to music and laughter
Welcome to the leaves on the tree

Welcome to the miracle of words
Welcome to the whispering of rivers

Welcome to dreaming
Welcome to everything you can see and name

Welcome to your mother's care
Welcome to your father's smile

Welcome to the love of all here
Welcome to the world

Selina Denton (1945–)

Portrait of a Child

Unconscious of amused and tolerant eyes,
He sits among his scattered dreams, and plays.
True to no one thing long; running for praise
With something less than half begun. He tries
To build his blocks against the furthest skies.
They fall; his soldiers tumble; but he stays
And plans and struts and laughs at fresh dismays –
Too confident and busy to be wise.

His toys are towns and temples: his commands
Bring forth vast armies trembling at his nod.
He shapes and shatters with impartial hands . . .
And, in his crude and tireless play, I see
The savage, the creator, and the god –
All that man was and all he hopes to be.

Louis Untermeyer (1885–1977)

'Time now makes a new beginning'

Time now makes a new beginning.
The world is both outside and inside.
 Live with our love.

At this moment there is no past
And consciousness is everywhere.
 Live with our love.

The world is both outside and inside
And now the worlds must be united.
 Live with our love.

And consciousness is everywhere
Of newly integrated spaces.
 Live with our love.

And now the worlds must be united
Into a manifold of being.
 Live with our love.

Of newly integrated spaces
What shall we say except that they
 Live with our love?

Into a manifold of being
Time now makes its new beginning.
 Live with our love, with our love.

   from 'Birth Bells for Louisa',
    John Fuller (1937–)

'Like a fish out of God's hand'

Like a fish out of God's hand
she fell and looked for her element,

the prints of her fingers
felt through the scales,

the warmth of her hand came up
like a gulf stream

and she swam,
over the galaxies, over the star trails,

over the moon and the borders of cloud
into my hand,

and she beat there like a fish not caught,
knowing everything water,

and I thought, how can I live up to it,
how can I catch from the hand of God

this fish, and while I was thinking
she slipped out

and made her own way into sea,
even without any water.

Desmond Graham (1940–)

'Her eyes the glow-worm lend thee'

Her eyes the glow-worm lend thee,
The shooting stars attend thee;
   And the elves also,
   Whose little eyes glow
Like the sparks of fire, befriend thee.

No Will-o'-the-Wisp mislight thee;
Nor snake, or slow-worms bite thee;
   But on, on thy way
   Not making a stay,
Since ghost there's none to affright thee.

Let not the dark thee cumber;
What though the moon does slumber?
   The stars of the night
   Will lend thee their light,
Like tapers clear without number.

from 'The Night-Piece, to Julia',
Robert Herrick (1591–1674)

Where am I going? . . .

Speak when ye're spoken tae,
Dae what ye're bidden,
Come when ye're ca'd,
And ye'll no be chidden.

Scottish Rhyme

Spring Morning

Where am I going? I don't quite know.
Down to the stream where the king-cups grow –
Up on the hill where the pine-trees blow –
Anywhere, anywhere. *I* don't know.

Where am I going? The clouds sail by,
Little ones, baby ones, over the sky.
Where am I going? The shadows pass,
Little ones, baby ones, over the grass.

If you were a cloud, and sailed up there,
You'd sail on water as blue as air,
And you'd see me here in the fields and say:
'Doesn't the sky look green to-day?'

Where am I going? The high rooks call:
'It's awful fun to be born at all.'
Where am I going? The ring-doves coo:
'We do have beautiful things to do.'

If you were a bird, and lived on high
You'd lean on the wind when the wind came by,
You'd say to the wind when it took you away:
'*That's* where I wanted to go to-day!'

Where am I going? I don't quite know.
What does it matter where people go?
Down to the wood where the blue-bells grow –
Anywhere, anywhere. *I* don't know.

A. A. Milne (1882–1956)

Baby Song

From the private ease of Mother's womb
I fall into the lighted room.

Why don't they simply put me back
Where it is warm and wet and black?

But one thing follows on another.
Things were different inside Mother.

Padded and jolly I would ride
The perfect comfort of her inside.

They tuck me in a rustling bed
– I lie there, raging, small, and red.

I may sleep soon. I may forget.
But I won't forget that I regret.

A rain of blood poured round her womb.
But all time roars outside this room.

Thom Gunn (1929–2004)

Isn't My Name Magical?

Nobody can see my name on me.
My name is inside
and all over me, unseen
like other people also keep it.
Isn't my name magical?

My name is mine only.
It tells I am individual,
the one special person it shakes
when I'm wanted.

Even if someone else answers
for me, my message hangs in air
haunting others, till it stops
with me, the right name.
Isn't your name and my name magic?

If I'm with hundreds of people
and my name gets called,
my sound switches me on to answer
like it was my human electricity.

My name echoes across playground,
it comes, it demands my attention.
I have to find out who calls,
who wants me for what.
My name gets blurted out in class,
it is terror, at a bad time,
because somebody is cross.

My name gets called in a whisper
I am happy, because
my name may have touched me
with a loving voice.
Isn't your name and my name magic?

James Berry (1924–)

Height

When I was young I felt so small
And frightened for the world was tall.

And even grasses seemed to me
A forest of immensity.

Until I learned that I could grow,
A glance would leave them far below.

Spanning a tree's height with my eye,
Suddenly I soared as high,

And fixing on a star I grew,
I pushed my head against the blue!

Still, like a singing lark, I find
Rapture to leave the grass behind.

And sometimes standing in a crowd
My lips are cool against a cloud.

Anne Morrow Lindbergh (1906–2001)

Being

I sat still and saw in my memory
Sunlight sheen between blades of green
Reminding me of a carefree childhood, Lord.
Sun filled, fun filled day after day with
Freedom to roam, a welcoming home.
Friends to share, compare our make believe in trust.
Knowing, showing life is for living, fully in action,
Days that were long and belonged to joy,
Magical moments the components of delight.
A touch of mystery, history of the moment's fresh pleasure.
For being, seeing each new adventure
Found, would abound in laughter's mirth.

Parents caring, sharing my growth.
Protecting, gently correcting out of love.
Nurturing, encouraging with the wisdom
Of years which appears and indeed does,
Bless, caress my family's existence.
So much to live for, give thanks for.
Good times behind and reaching ahead in hope.
Memories growing fonder, wander down
The labyrinth of my mind where I find
Always more reason each and every season
To bring You the heartfelt gratitude of praise,
As I claim, name the marvel of being alive.

Sue O'Donnell

The joys of motherhood . . .

My baby has a mottle fist,
My baby has a neck in creases;
My baby kisses and is kissed,
For he's the very thing for kisses.

Christina Rossetti (1830–94)

On Being a Mum

The joys of motherhood it's said
Are when they're tucked up safe in bed.
Our little treasures seem to be
Afflicted with perversity
When naught you do can quell their noise –
And girls are just as bad as boys.
'Go to your room!' a hopeless threat
Which all too soon you may regret.
For in the tip that is their room
There's a deathly silence like the tomb.
What are they doing? Are they there?
A quiet house is very rare . . .
Savour the moment – your breath regain,
Before too long it starts again!
The arguments; the endless huff;
A ploy they try to call your bluff.
They make you angry; they think you're dumb
Then a sudden smile and 'I love you, Mum.'
What can you do? What can you say?
They're your bairns and they steal your heart away.

Vivian Finlay

The Victory

I thought you were my victory
though you cut me like a knife
when I brought you out of my body
into your life.

Tiny antagonist, gory,
blue as a bruise. The stains
of your cloud of glory
bled from my veins.

How can you dare, blind thing,
blank insect eyes?
You barb the air. You sting
with bladed cries.

Snail! Scary knot of desires!
Hungry snarl! Small son.
Why do I have to love you?
How have you won?

Anne Stevenson (1933–)

46

'What did my fingers do before they held him?'

What did my fingers do before they held him?
What did my heart do, with its love?
I have never seen a thing so clear.
His lids are like the lilac-flower
and soft as a moth, his breath.
I shall not let go.
There is no guile or warp in him. May he keep so.

*

I shall meditate upon normality.
I shall meditate upon my little son.
He does not walk. He does not speak a word.
He is still swaddled in white bands.
But he is pink and perfect. He smiles so frequently.
I have papered his room with big roses,
I have painted little hearts on everything.

I do not will him to be exceptional.
It is the exception that interests the devil.
It is the exception that climbs the sorrowful hill
Or sits in the desert and hurts his mother's heart.
I will him to be common,
To love me as I love him,
And to marry what he wants and where he will.

from 'Three Women', *Sylvia Plath* (1932–63)

Love Me

Love me . . . I love you,
   Love me, my baby;
Sing it high, sing it low,
   Sing it as may be.

Mother's arms under you,
   Her eyes above you
Sing it high, sing it low,
   Love me . . . I love you.

Christina Rossetti (1830–94)

Now that I am Forever with Child

How the days went
while you were blooming within me
I remember each upon each –
the swelling changed planes of my body
and how you first fluttered, then jumped
and I thought it was my heart.

How the days wound down
and the turning of winter
I recall with you growing heavy
against the wind. I thought
now her hands
are formed, and her hair
has started to curl
now her teeth are done
now she sneezes.
Then the seed opened
I bore you one morning just before spring
My head rang like a fiery piston
my legs were towers between which
A new world was passing.

Since then
I can only distinguish
one thread within running hours
You, flowing through selves
toward You.

Audre Lorde (1934–1992)

Love & Milk

Not knowing even if you like me
   I give you milk . . . and love,
Though roughly in equal proportions,
My breasts and my heart overflowing
   for your survival.
Drawing back so as not to choke you
   with their goodness.

And giving
has become a blur
            of day and night
   and wet and dry
   and sleep and cry,
Punctuated by my warm arms
And your bright frowning eyes
      that give the lie
   to those who say you cannot yet see.
So here   in this womb of a dishevelled bed
         You   and   me,
Indulging again in
   Milk and love
      Habitually.

Krista Dickson

Mirroring

Now he lies asleep, after the fury,
the blue of his eyelids luminous
in the cool dark;
then, one hot arm thrown across his face
as if to bar me from his dreams
dilates my eyes with tears:
this was how you slept,
this gesture so defiant
in its suffering.

You are reflections
shattering and remaking:
I remember the hot white light of birth
the searing joy as he flew,
long, slithery fish,
up out of my cut flesh,
as a soul leaves a body.
I remember the slow, brave wasting of your life
across the summer, which felt like a birth to me.

I see you in his face, my mother, as if
your breath touched him and left life there
As if I am the mirror,
and janus-eyed I offer him to you
and offer you to him

and these shards of glass in me
are fierce birthpains
bringing love, again,
to life.

Pippa Little

Song for a Young Mother

There, there, you fit my lap
Like an acorn to its cup,
Your weight upon my arm
Is like a golden plum,
Like an apple in the hand
Or a stone on the ground.

As a bird in the fallow
scoops a shallow hollow
Where the earth's upward pressing
Answers egg and nestling
– Earth's mass and beginning
Of all their learning –

So you learn from my arm
You have substance and a house
So I learn from your birth
that I am not vague and wild
But as solid as my child
And as constant as the earth.

E. J. Scovell (1907–99)

To Our Daughter

And she is beautiful, our daughter.
Only six months, but a person.
She turns to look at everything, out walking.
All so precious. I mustn't disturb it with words.
People are like great clowns,
Blossom like balloons, black pigeons like eagles,
Water beyond belief.

She holds out her hand to air,
Sea, sky, wind, sun, movement, stillness,
And wants to hold them all.
My finger is her earth connection, me, and earth.

Her head is like an apple, or an egg.
Skin stretched fine over a strong casing,
Her whole being developing from within
And from without: the answer.

And she sings, long notes from the belly or the throat,
Her legs kick her feet up to her nose,
She rests – laid still like a large rose.
She is our child,
The world is not hers, she has to win it.

Jenifer Armitage

Love Affair

Some day he'll think me rather silly,
But now he loves me willy-nilly.

There'll come a time when his inspection
Will tell him I am not perfection.

And he'll unearth some younger cutie
Who far surpasses me in beauty.

So while I have him in my arms
I'll make the most of all my charms.

And store up memories to last
When I am dwelling in the past.

For though my hold on him is strong,
He cannot stay a baby long.

Margaret Fishback (1904–85)

Like Mother, Like Son

Do you know that your soul is of my soul such a part,
That you seem to be fibre and core of my heart?
None other can pain me as you, dear, can do,
None other can please me or praise me as you.

Remember the world will be quick with its blame
If shadow or stain ever darken your name.
'Like mother, like son' is a saying so true
The world will judge largely the 'mother' by you.

Be yours then the task, if task it shall be,
To force the proud world to do homage to me.
Be sure it will say, when its verdict you've won,
'She reaped as she sowed. Lo! this is her son.'

Margaret Johnston Grafflin

Mother Love

As a rainbow glows
As a flower grows
As a river flows
As the warm wind blows

Such is a mother's love

As the sea is deep
As a hill is steep
As a deer might leap

Such is a mother's love

As a lion roars
As an eagle soars

Such is a mother's love.

Traditional,
adapted by Claire Beddowes (1953–)

Giving Birth

Delivering this gift
requires blood,
a remote room,
the presence of overseers.

They tug a child
out of the ruins of your flesh.

Birth is not given.
It is what is taken from you;
not a gift you give
but a tax levied on you.

Not a gift but a bout
that ages both the contestants.

Birthshocks hold on tight, for years,
like hooked bristles of goosegrass,
cleavers clinging to your skirt and sleeves.

The raw mime of labour
is never healed,
in giving birth
the women's innocence goes,
loss you can't brush away,
it stains all your new clothes.

No longer can you be half-woman, half-bird.
Now you are all woman,
you are all given away,
your child has the wings,
can resist the pull of the earth.

You watch her rush up,
clowning her way through the cloud.

And you applaud.

Penelope Shuttle (1947–)

'I had expected so little'

The midwife asked me if I would like to see the child. 'Please,' I said gratefully, and she went away and came back with my daughter wrapped up in a small grey bloodstained blanket, and with a ticket saying 'Stacey' round her ankle. She put her in my arms and I sat there looking at her, and her great wide blue eyes looked at me with seeming recognition, and what I felt it is pointless to try to describe. Love, I suppose one might call it, and the first of my life.

I had expected so little, really. I never expect much. I had been told of the ugliness of newborn children, of their red and wrinkled faces, their waxy covering, their emaciated limbs, their hairy cheeks, their piercing cries. All I can say is that mine was beautiful and in my defence I must add that others said she was beautiful too. She was not red nor even wrinkled, but palely soft, each feature delicately reposed in its right place, and she was not bald but adorned with a thick, startling crop of black hair. One of the nurses fetched a brush and flattened it down and it covered her forehead, lying in a dense fringe that reached to her eyes. And her eyes, that seemed to see me and that looked into mine with deep gravity and charm, were a profound blue, the whites white with the gleam of alarming health. When they asked if they could have her back and put her back in her cradle for the night, I handed her over without reluctance, for the delight of holding her was too much for me. I felt as well as they that such pleasure should be regulated and rationed.

from *The Millstone*, Margaret Drabble (1939–)

Creation

You were made
under the sea
your ear gives you away.

You were made
in the calyx of a rose
your skin betrays you.

You were made in heaven
your eyelids as you sleep
cannot disguise themselves.

You were brought to me
by a giant kite
his wings stir white

on my face still.
Never say you grew
from a seed in my body

the dandelion brought you
the spring brought you
a star with brilliant hands

delivered you
leaving his light in your eyes
as a seal, and a promise.

Jeni Couzyn (1942–)

60

'Two little feet, so small that both may nestle'

Two little feet, so small that both may nestle
   In one caressing hand –
Two tender feet upon the untried border
   Of life's mysterious land.

Dimpled, and soft, and pink as peach-tree blossoms,
   In April's fragrant days,
How can they walk among the briery tangles,
   Edging the world's rough ways?

These rose-white feet, along the doubtful future,
   Must bear a mother's load;
Alas! since Woman has the heaviest burden,
   And walks the harder road.

Love, for a while, will make the path before them
   All dainty, smooth and fair   –
Will cull away the brambles, letting only
   The roses blossom there.

But when the mother's watchful eyes are shrouded
   Away from sight of men,
And these dear feet are left without her guiding,
   Who shall direct them then?

*

Ah! who may read the future? for our darling
   We crave all blessings sweet,
And pray that He who feeds the crying ravens
   Will guide the baby's feet.

From 'Little Feet', *Elizabeth Akers* (1832–1911)

Lullaby for a First Child

This timid gift I nurse
as the one clear thing I can do.
I am new and history-less
as the name on your wrist, as you.
But flesh has stored a deep kindness
ready to welcome you.
Take it, a little silver
into your small purse.
There it will gather interest
– the warm, bright weight of you.

Carol Rumens (1944–)

The joys of fatherhood . . .

This above all: to thine own self be true,
And it must follow, as the night the day,
Thou canst not then be false to any man.

from *Hamlet* (I, iii), William Shakespeare (1564–1616)

To Ianthe

I love thee, Baby! For thine own sweet sake;
   Those azure eyes, that faintly dimpled cheek.
   Thy tender frame, so eloquently weak,
   Love in the sternest heart of hate might wake;
But more when o'er thy fitful slumber bending
   Thy mother folds thee to her wakeful heart,
   Whilst love and pity, in her glances bending,
   All that thy passive eyes can feel impart:
More, when some feeble lineaments of her,
   Who bore thy weight beneath her spotless bosom,
   As with deep love I read thy face, recur! –
More dear art thou, O fair and fragile blossom;
   Dearest when most thy tender traits express
   The image of thy mother's loveliness.

Percy Bysshe Shelley (1792–1822)

To My Daughter

Bright clasp of her whole hand around my finger,
My daughter, as we walk together now,
All my life I'll feel a ring invisibly
Circle this bone with shining: when she is grown
Far from today as her eyes are far already.

Stephen Spender (1909–95)

'She was born in the autumn'

She was born in the autumn and was a late fall in my life, and lay purple and dented like a little bruised plum, as though she'd been lightly trodden in the grass and forgotten.

Then the nurse lifted her up and she came suddenly alive, her bent legs kicking crabwise, and her first living gesture was a thin wringing of the hands accompanied by a far-out Hebridean lament.

This moment of meeting seemed to be a birthtime for both of us; her first and my second life. Nothing, I knew, would be the same again, and I think I was reasonably shaken. I peered intently at her, looking for familiar signs, but she was convulsed as an Aztec idol. Was this really my daughter, this purple concentration of anguish, this blind and protesting dwarf?

When they handed her to me, stiff and howling, and I held her for the first time and kissed her, and she went still and quiet as though by instinctive guile, and I was instantly enslaved by her flattery of my powers . . .

Now this girl, my child, this parcel of will and warmth, fills the cottage with her obsessive purpose. The rhythmic tides of her sleeping and feeding spaciously measure the days and nights. Her frail self-absorption is a commanding presence, her helplessness strong as a rock, so that I find myself listening even to her silences as though some great engine was purring upstairs.

When I watch her at this I see her hauling in life, groping fiercely with every limb and muscle, working blind at a task no one can properly share, in a darkness where she is still alone.

She is of course just an ordinary miracle, but is also the particular late wonder of my life.

Here she is then, my daughter, here, alive, the one I must possess and guard. A year ago this space was empty, not even a hope of her was in it. Now she's here, brand new, with our name upon her: and no one will call in the night to reclaim her.

from *The Firstborn*, Laurie Lee (1914–1997)

The Birthnight: To F.

(The poet's daughter, Florence)

Dearest, it was a night
That in its darkness rocked Orion's stars;
A sighing wind ran faintly white
Along the willows, and the cedar boughs
Laid their wide hands in stealthy peace across
The starry silence of their antique moss:
No sound save rushing air
Cold, yet all sweet with Spring,
And in thy mother's arms, crouched weeping there,
    Thou, lovely thing.

Walter de la Mare (1873–1956)

'I should never again have an easy hour'

Monday, 9 October 1775

My wife having been seized with her pains in the night, I got up about three o'clock, and between four and five Dr Young came. He and I sat upstairs mostly till between three and four, when, after we had dined, her labour became violent. I was full of expectation, and meditated curiously on the thought that it was already certain of what sex the child was, but that I could not have the least guess on which side the probability was . . . I did not feel so much anxiety about my wife now as on former occasions, being better used to an inlying. Yet the danger was as great now as ever. I was easier from the same deception which affects a soldier who has escaped in several battles. She was very ill. Between seven and eight I went into the room. She was just delivered. I heard her say, 'God be thanked for whatever he sends.' I supposed then the child was a daughter. But she herself had not then seen it. Miss Preston said, 'Is it a daughter?' 'No,' said Mrs Forrest, the nurse-keeper, 'it's a son.' When I had seen the little man I said that I should now be so anxious that probably I should never again have an easy hour. I said to Dr Young with great seriousness, 'Doctor, Doctor, let no man set his heart upon anything in this world but land or heritable bonds; for he has no security that anything else will last as long as himself.' My anxiety subdued a flutter of joy which was in my breast. I wrote several letters to announce my son's birth. I indulged some imaginations that he might perhaps be a great man.

from his *Diary*, James Boswell (1740–95)

For Milena

(aged 2)

I would take you into my arms rolled up
like an astrolabe, ribbed and bound with love
impregnable and you would beat your hand prints
on the inside smoked, coming out like a chick's
beak or turtle tot, splitting my sides

I would take you into my bathysphere, well-cased
and riveted to any depth, curling my whole weight
like nesting birds around you, hurdling you in
with tideless favour so the deep sea's swell
would be no more than breath on a window
blown for writing names, but you would crack
the embrasure, stride out like a new born armadillo
from its shell, bison worried at the water line,
porpoise from the net of sea, surfaced into air

I would hold you in a ring of talking soft enough
to suck cream with, spell all around the oaths
of surety which not a witch or gorgon
taking a brickbat stroll could launch through,
iron ribbed in feeling, haversacked in love,
safe from the outside and you would walk easy –
as you did from the first room with your eyes
slipping over mine to mother's and then on
to the great outside of walls and windows –
arms swinging, legs astride the world and moving,
your roller ball, into whatever.

Desmond Graham (1940–)

To a New Baby

Little kicking, cuddling thing,
You don't cry – you only sing!
Blinking eyes and stubby nose,
Mouth that mocks the budding rose,
Down for hair, peach-blows for hands . . .
Ah-h-h-h! Of all the "baby-grands"
Anyone could wish to see,
You're the finest one for me!

Skin as soft as velvet is;
God (when you were only his)
Touched you on the cheek and chin –
Where he touched are dimples in.
Creases on your wrists, as though
Strings were fastened 'round them so
We could tie you tight and keep
You from leaving while we sleep.

Once I tried to look at you
From a stranger's point of view;
You were red and wrinkled; then
I just loved, and looked again;
What I saw was not the same;
In my eyes the blessed flame
Of a father's love consumed
Faults to strangers' eyes illumed.

Little squirming, cuddling thing!
Ere you shed each angel wing,
Did they tell you you were sent
With a cargo of content

To a home down here below
Where they hungered for you so?
Do you know, you flawless pearl,
How we love our baby girl?

Strickland W. Gillilan (1869–1954)

Waking with Russell

Whatever the difference is, it all began
the day we woke up face-to-face like lovers
and his four-day-old smile dawned on him again,
possessed him, till it would not fall or waver;
and I pitched back not my old hard-pressed grin
but his own smile, or one I'd rediscovered.
Dear son, I was *mezzo del cammin*
and the true path was as lost to me as ever
when you cut in front and lit it as you ran.
See how the true gift never leaves the giver:
returned and redelivered, it rolled on
until the smile poured through us like a river.
How fine, I thought, this waking amongst men!
I kissed your mouth and pledged myself forever.

Don Paterson (1963–)

'Once more the storm is howling'

Once more the storm is howling, and half hid
Under this cradle-hood and coverlid
My child sleeps on. There is no obstacle
But Gregory's wood and one bare hill
Whereby the haystack- and roof-levelling wind,
Bred on the Atlantic, can be stayed;
And for an hour I have walked and prayed
Because of the great gloom that is in my mind.

I have walked and prayed for this young child an hour
And heard the sea-wind scream upon the tower,
And under the arches of the bridge, and scream
In the elms above the flooded stream;
Imagining in excited reverie
That the future years had come,
Dancing to a frenzied drum,
Out of the murderous innocence of the sea.

May she be granted beauty and yet not
Beauty to make a stranger's eye distraught,
Or hers before a looking-glass, for such,
Being made beautiful overmuch,
Consider beauty a sufficient end,
Lose natural kindness and maybe
The heart-revealing intimacy
That chooses right, and never find a friend . . .

In courtesy I'd have her chiefly learned;
Hearts are not had as a gift but hearts are earned
By those that are not entirely beautiful;
Yet many, that have played the fool

For beauty's very self, has charm made wise,
And many a poor man that has roved,
Loved and thought himself beloved,
From a glad kindness cannot take his eyes.

May she become a flourishing hidden tree
That all her thoughts may like the linnet be,
And have no business but dispensing round
Their magnanimities of sound,
Nor but in merriment begin a chase,
Nor but in merriment a quarrel.
O may she live like some green laurel
Rooted in one dear perpetual place.

from 'A Prayer for My Daughter',
W. B. Yeats (1865–1939)

'What have I got exactly?'

What have I got exactly? And what am I going to do with her? And what for that matter will she do with me?

I have got a daughter, whose life is already separate from mine, whose will already follows its own directions, and who has quickly corrected my woolly preconceptions of her by being something remorselessly different. She is the child of herself and will be what she is. I am merely the keeper of her temporary helplessness.

Even so, with luck, she can alter me; indeed, is doing so now.

But if I could teach her anything at all – by unloading upon her some of the ill-tied parcels of my years – I'd like it to be acceptance and a holy relish for life. To accept with gladness the fact of being a woman – when she'll find all nature to be on her side.

If pretty, to thank God and enjoy her luck and not start beefing about being loved for her mind. To be willing to give pleasure without feeling loss of face, to prefer charm to the vanity of aggression, and not to deliver her powers and mysteries into the opposite camp by wishing to compete with men.

In this way, I believe – though some of her sisters may disapprove – she might know some happiness and also spread some around.

And as a brief tenant of this precious and irreplaceable world, I'd ask her to preserve life both in herself and others. To prefer always Societies for Propagation and Promotion rather than those for the Abolition or Prevention of.

Never to persecute others for the sins hidden in herself, nor to seek justice in terms of vengeance; to avoid like a plague all acts of mob-righteousness; to take cover whenever flags start flying; and to accept her faults and frustrations as her own personal burden, and not to blame them too often, if she can possibly help it, on young or old, whites or coloureds, East, West, Jews, Gentiles, Television, Bingo, Trades Unions, the City, school-milk, or the British Railways.

For the rest, may she be my own salvation, for any man's child is his second chance. In this role I see her leading me back to my beginnings, reopening rooms I'd locked and forgotten, stirring the dust in my mind by re-asking the big questions – as any child can do.

But in my case, perhaps, just not too late; she persuades me there may yet be time, that with her, my tardy but bright-eyed pathfinder, I may return to that wood which long ago I fled from, but which together we may now enter and know.

from *The Firstborn* Laurie Lee (1914–1997)

Baby Feet

Tell me, what is half so sweet
As a baby's tiny feet,
Pink and dainty as can be,
Like a coral from the sea?
Talk of jewels strung in rows,
Gaze upon those little toes,
Fairer than a diadem,
With the mother kissing them!

It is morning and she lies
Uttering her happy cries,
While her little hands reach out
For the feet that fly about.
Then I go to her and blow
Laughter out of every toe;
Hold her high and let her place
Tiny footprints on my face.

Little feet that do not know
Where the winding roadways go,
Little feet that never tire,
Feel the stones or trudge the mire,
Still too pink and still too small
To do anything but crawl,
Thinking all their wanderings fair,
Filled with wonders everywhere.

Little feet, so rich with charm,
May you never come to harm.
As I bend and proudly blow
Laughter out of every toe,

This I pray, that God above
Shall protect you with His love,
And shall guide those little feet
Safely down life's broader street.

Edgar A. Guest (1881–1959)

To a Child

My fairest child, I have no song to sing thee;
No lark could pipe in skies so dull and grey;
Yet, if thou wilt, one lesson I will give thee
For every day.

Be good, sweet maid, and let who can be clever;
Do lovely things, not dream them, all day long;
And so make Life, Death, and that vast For Ever
One grand sweet song.

Charles Kingsley (1819–75)

The finest baby in the world . . .

When the first baby laughed for the first time the laugh broke into a thousand pieces and they all went skipping about and that was the beginning of the fairies.

J. M. Barrie (1860–1937)

'The Finest Baby in the World'

The door opened, and Merle found herself in a long room. It was almost entirely filled with babies' cradles.

Babies' cradles of every description! Some quite grand ones, trimmed with rows of ribbon and lace, so grand that you would never have thought of giving them such a simple name as cradle, but would have at once decided that they were 'bassinettes'. Some quite ordinary basket cradles, some old-fashioned wooden ones that had evidently been used for more than one generation of babies, and some not proper cradles at all. One was an old tin bath, another a big basket, and another a wooden box . . .

She was most devoted to any baby; she loved the whole baby race, as every girl should do, and, in fact, as every right-minded girl does.

Well, Merle peeped into the first cradle. It happened to be one of the grandly trimmed ones. In it was lying a very small, very thin, very pale, but very clean baby. Any one who was not fond of babies would have said, 'What an ugly baby!' Merle only thought, 'That poor baby looks ill!'

There was a ticket fastened to one of the curtains. On the ticket was written – Merle looked twice, she thought she must have made a mistake; but no, there it was plainly written, 'The Finest Baby in the World'.

She was rather astonished, for she felt sure that she had seen finer babies many a time.

In the next cradle – the tin bath one – lay a very bonnie baby, also wide-awake and perfectly happy. This was quite a different-looking baby. It had rosy cheeks and curly hair, though rather a dirty face. It really was a fine baby. Merle saw a ticket fastened to this cradle, and when she looked at it, she saw written on that too, 'The Finest Baby in the World'.

Then she looked at the next cradle, and on that was another ticket with exactly the same words on it. She looked at another, and another, and another – it was just the same all the way round – every baby, pretty or plain, clean or dirty, thin or fat, each one was labelled, 'The Finest Baby in the World'.

Merle stood bewildered. What could it all mean?

'It is simple nonsense!' she said aloud. 'There can be only one *finest* baby in the whole world.'

'That's just the point . . .' Standing close beside her was a small boy who looked about three years old, but who spoke as if he were very much older.

'Just it,' he repeated decidedly; 'that's just what we want to find out, which is the finest?'

Merle stared at him, amazed . . . 'How is it that all these babies are labelled "The Finest Baby in the World"? Who gave them their labels?'

'Their mothers, of course,' said Thomas Muriel.

from *Wanted – A King*, Maggie Browne

Choosing a Name

I have got a new-born sister;
I was nigh the first that kissed her.
When the nursing woman brought her
To papa, his infant daughter,
How papa's dear eye did glisten!
She will shortly be to christen:
And papa has made the offer,
I shall have the naming of her.

Now I wonder what would please her,
Charlotte, Julia, or Louisa.
Ann and Mary, they're too common;
Joan's too formal for a woman;
Jane's a prettier name beside;
But we had a Jane that died.
They would say, if 'twas Rebecca,
That she was a little Quaker.
Edith's pretty, but that looks
Better in old English books;
Ellen's left off long ago;
Blanche is out of fashion now.
None that I have named as yet
Are so good as Margaret.
Emily is neat and fine.
What do you think of Caroline?
How I'm puzzled and perplexed
What to choose or think of next!

I am in a little fever,
Lest the name that I shall give her
Should disgrace her or defame her,
I will leave papa to name her.

Charles and Mary Lamb
(1775–1834 and 1765–1847)

Which Day are you?

Monday's child is fair of face,
Tuesday's child is full of grace,
Wednesday's child is full of woe,
Thursday's child has far to go.
Friday's child is loving and giving,
Saturday's child works hard for a living,
And the child that is born on the Sabbath, they say,
Is bonny and blithe and bright as the day.

Traditional

Variations on a Theme

Monday's child is fair of face
And we will always say so.
Dare declare the child is fair
And will always stay so.

Tuesday's child is full of grace
So you might think he knows his place
Not so – he has the grace to say
Don't do things your way, do them my way.

Wednesday's child is full of woe
So we assume he's feeling low
Not so – he's up for fun and play
Every day *except* Wednesday.

Thursday's child has far to go –
Though all he does is cry and feed.
Maybe, in a year or so,
He'll quieten down and pick up speed.

Friday's child is loving and giving
Which is evident all right.
He's only recently started living
And he loves to give you sleepless nights!

Saturday's child works hard for a living
But, being rather clever,
Marries the one that's loving and giving
And then stops work for ever.

A child that is born on the Sabbath, they say,
Is bonny and blithe and bright as the day.
If you've got one of those – well, fine.
If not, you'd better try again.

Megan Brookes (1968–)

Mighty Like a Rose

Sweetest little feller,
Everybody knows;
Don't know what to call him,
But he's mighty like a rose.

Looking at his Mammy
With eyes so shiny blue,
Make you think that heaven
Is coming close to you.

Frank L. Stanton (1857–1927)

The End

When I was One,
I had just begun.

When I was Two,
I was nearly new.

When I was Three,
I was hardly Me.

When I was Four,
I was not much more.

When I was Five,
I was just alive.

But now I am Six, I'm as clever as clever.
So I think I'll be six now for ever and ever.

A. A. Milne (1882–1956)

Christopher Milne on A. A. Milne

My father, who had derived such happiness from his childhood, found in me the companion with whom he could return there. But with Nanny in the way he could only take his dream son and return in imagination – to mend a train or keep a dormouse or go fishing. When I was three he was three. When I was six he was six. We grew up side by side and as we grew so the books were written. Then when I was nine and he was nine Nanny left. We could now do real things together: reality could in part replace the dream. For the next nine years we continued to grow up alongside each other. I was not aware of this, of course. I just saw him as my father. But he, I now suspect, saw me as a sort of twin brother, perhaps a sort of reincarnation of Ken. I – as I have already mentioned – needed him. He no less but for a different reason needed me. He needed me to escape from being fifty.

A Parental Ode to My Son, Aged Three Years and Five Months

Thou happy, happy elf!
(But stop. – first let me kiss away that tear) –
Thou tiny image of myself!
(My love, he's poking peas into his ear!)
Thou merry, laughing sprite!
With spirits feather-light,
Untouched by sorrow, and unsoiled by sin –
(Good heavens! the child is swallowing a pin!)

Thou little tricksy Puck!
With antic toys so funnily bestuck,
Light as the singing bird that wings the air –
(The door! the door! he'll tumble down the stair!)
Thou darling of thy sire!
(Why, Jane, he'll set his pinafore a-fire!)
Thou imp of mirth and joy!
In Love's dear chain so strong and bright a link,
Thou idol of thy parents – (Drat the boy!
There goes my ink!)

Thou cherub – but of earth;
Fit playfellow for Fays, by moonlight pale.
In harmless sport and mirth,
(That dog will bite him if he pulls its tail!)
Thou human humming-bee extracting honey
From ev'ry blossom in the world that blows,
Singing in Youth's Elysium ever sunny,
(Another tumble! – that's his precious nose!)
Thy father's pride and hope!
(He'll break the mirror with that skipping-rope!)

With pure heart newly stamped from Nature's mint –
(Where did he learn that squint?)

        Thou young domestic dove!
(He'll have that jug off, with another shove!)
      Dear nursling of the hymeneal nest!
        (Are those torn clothes his best!)
        Little epitome of man!
(He'll climb upon the table, that's his plan!)
Touched with the beauteous tints of dawning life –
         (He's got a knife!)

        Thou enviable being!
No storms, no clouds, in thy blue sky foreseeing,
        Play on, play on.
        My elfin John!
Toss the light ball – bestride the stick –
(I knew so many cakes would make him sick!)
With fancies buoyant as the thistle down,
Prompting the face grotesque, and antic brisk,
        With many a lamb-like frisk,
(He's got the scissors, snipping at your gown!)

        Thou pretty opening rose!
(Go to your mother, child, and wipe your nose!)
Balmy, and breathing music like the South,
(He really brings my heart into my mouth!)
Fresh as the morn, and brilliant as its star –
(I wish that window had an iron bar!)
Bold as the hawk, yet gentle as the dove –
        (I tell you what my love,
I cannot write, unless he's sent above!)

Thomas Hood (1798–1845)

'The use of knowledge'

You should encourage your daughter to talk over with you what she reads; and as you are very capable of distinguishing, take care she does not mistake pert folly for wit and humour, or rhyme for poetry, which are the common errors of young people, and have a train of ill consequences. The second caution to be given her (and which is most absolutely necessary) is to conceal whatever learning she attains, with as much solicitude as she would hide crookedness or lameness: the parade of it can only serve to draw on her the envy, and consequently the most inveterate hatred, of all he and she fools, which will certainly be at least three parts in four her acquaintance. The use of knowledge in our sex, beside the amusement of solitude, is to moderate the passions, and learn to be contented with a small expense, which are the certain effects of a studious life: and it may be preferable even to that fame which men have engrossed to themselves, and will not suffer us to share. You will tell me I have not observed this rule myself; but you are mistaken: it is only inevitable accident that has given me any reputation that way. I have always carefully avoided it, and ever thought it a misfortune. The explanation of this paragraph would occasion a long digression, which I will not trouble you with, it being my present design only to say what I think useful for the instruction of my granddaughter, which I have much at heart. If she has the same inclination (I should say passion) for learning that I was born with, history, geography, and philosophy will furnish her with materials to pass away cheerfully a longer life that is allotted to mortals. I believe there are few heads capable of making Sir Isaac Newton's calculations, but the result of them is not difficult to be understood by a moderate capacity.

from a letter to the Countess of Bute, 28 January 1753,
Lady Mary Wortley Montagu (1689–1762)

'Child, when they say that others'

Child, when they say that others
    Have been or are like you,
Babes fit to be your brothers,
    Sweet human drops of dew,
Bright fruit of mortal mothers,
    What should one say or do?

We know the thought is treason,
    We feel the dream absurd;
A claim rebuked of reason,
    That withers at a word:
For never shone the season
    That bore so blithe a bird.

Some smiles may seem as merry,
    Some glances gleam as wise,
From lips as like a cherry
    And scarce less gracious eyes;
Eyes browner than a berry,
    Lips red as morning's rise.

But never yet rang laughter
    So sweet in gladdened ears
Through wall and floor and rafter
    As all this household bears
And rings response thereafter
    Till cloudiest weather clears.

*

The dawn were not more cheerless
   With neither light nor dew
Than we without the fearless
   Clear laugh that thrills us through:
If ever child stood peerless,
   Love knows that child is you.

                    from 'Comparisons',
Algernon Charles Swinburne (1837–1909)

Song to be Sung by the Father of Infant Female Children

My heart leaps up when I behold
A rainbow in the sky;
Contrariwise, my blood runs cold
When little boys go by.
For little boys as little boys,
No special hate I carry,
But now and then they grow to men,
And when they do, they marry.
No matter how they tarry,
Eventually they marry.
And, swine among the pearls,
They marry little girls.

Oh, somewhere, somewhere, an infant plays,
With parents who feed and clothe him.
Their lips are sticky with pride and praise,
But I have begun to loathe him.
Yes, I loathe with a loathing shameless
This child who to me is nameless.
This bachelor child in his carriage
Gives never a thought to marriage,
But a person can hardly say knife
Before he will hunt him a wife.

I never see an infant (male),
A-sleeping in the sun,
Without I turn a trifle pale
And think Is *he* the one?
Oh, first he'll want to crop his curls,
And then he'll want a pony,
And then he'll think of pretty girls

And holy matrimony.
He'll put away his pony,
And sigh for matrimony.
A cat without a mouse
Is he without a spouse.

Oh, somewhere he bubbles bubbles of milk,
And quietly sucks his thumbs.
His cheeks are roses painted on silk,
And his teeth are tucked in his gums.
But alas, the teeth will begin to grow,
And the bubbles will cease to bubble;
Given a score of years or so,
The roses will turn to stubble.
He'll sell a bond, or he'll write a book,
And his eyes will get that acquisitive look,
And raging and ravenous for the kill,
He'll boldly ask for the hand of Jill.
This infant whose middle
Is diapered still
Will want to marry
My daughter Jill.

Oh sweet be his slumber and moist his middle!
My dreams, I fear, are infanticiddle.
A fig for embryo Lohengrins!
I'll open all of his safety pins,
I'll pepper his powder, and salt his bottle,
And give him readings from Aristotle.
Sand for his spinach I'll gladly bring,
And Tabasco sauce for his teething ring.
Then perhaps he'll struggle though fire and water
To marry somebody else's daughter.

Ogden Nash (1902–71)

'Who do you think he is like?'

'Now, uncle,' said Mr Kitterbell, lifting that part of the mantle which covered the infant's face, with an air of great triumph, '*who* do you think he's like?'

'He! He! Yes, who?' said Mrs K., putting her arm through her husband's, and looking up into Dump's face with an expression of as much interest as she was capable of displaying.

'Good God, how small he is!' cried the amiable uncle, starting back with well-feigned surprise; '*remarkably* small indeed.'

'Do you think so?' inquired poor little Kitterbell, rather alarmed. 'He's a monster to what he was – ain't he, nurse?'

'He's a dear,' said the nurse, squeezing the child . . .

A general hum of admiration interrupted the conversation . . . An universal rush of the young ladies immediately took place. (Girls are always *so* fond of babies in company.)

'Oh, you dear!' said one.

'How sweet!' cried another, in a low tone of the most enthusiastic admiration.

'Heavenly!' added a third.

'Oh, what dear little arms!' said a fourth . . .

'Did you ever?' – said a little coquette with a large bustle, who looked like a French lithograph, appealing to a gentleman in three waistcoats – 'did you ever?'

'Never in my life,' returned her admirer, pulling up his collar.

'Oh! *do* let me take it, nurse,' cried another young lady. 'The love!'

'Can it open its eyes, nurse?' inquired another, affecting the utmost innocence. – Suffice it to say that the single ladies unanimously voted him an angel, and that the married ones, *nem.con.*, agreed that he was decidedly the finest baby they had ever beheld – except their own . . .

from 'The Bloomsbury Christening', *Sketches by Boz*,
Charles Dickens (1812–70)

Condolences of the Season

To my son (born December 1964)

And now it seems that you and I, my son,
must suffer with like fortitude
the diddums chorus, the ickle-man alleluia,
together with such other ritual oddments
as maiden aunt and grand-dam can devise . . .

                                        For months to come
your crabbed infant-elderly countenance
must be mulled over to the tea-cup's chink,
a matronly cosmogony of mums
hover above your pram or basinette
and by an infallible process of recall
place each distinctive trait (the eyes, for instance,
which could only be Uncle Tom's, nobody else's,
Aunt Lena's rugged chin, of course and, yes,
who could mistake those ears of Cousin Ted's?)

Identi-Kitted out as fulsomely
as the most Wanted criminal, any means
you choose to shake them off are bound to fail
– bearded, double-chinned, dark-spectacled,
the hair grown long and thatching tell-tale ears,
cheeks padded with the lard of middle-age
– you'll fancy the trail cold, the pack confused,
until, at a family reunion, some frail
octogenarian creature, screaming out,
'How could I be so foolish? Harry's nose!'
shaking with recognition pulls you down . . .

Lapped in a bunny-rug, you stare them out
and, smarter than they realize, play it dumb,
while, slung for burping purposes across
your mother's shoulder, all is well I see,
catching your droll heretical wink at me . . .

Bruce Dawe (1930–)

'Squaring at existence'

Dombey sat in the corner of the darkened room in the great armchair by the bedside, and Son lay tucked up warm in a little basket bedstead, carefully disposed on a low settee immediately in front of the fire and close to it, as if his constitution were analogous to that of a muffin, and it was essential to toast him brown while he was very new.

Dombey was about eight-and-forty years of age. Son about eight-and-forty minutes. Dombey was rather bald, rather red, and though a handsome well-made man, too stern and pompous in appearance to be prepossessing. Son was very bald, and very red, and though (of course) an undeniably fine infant, somewhat crushed and spotty in his general effect, as yet. On the brow of Dombey, Time and his brother Care had set some marks, as on a tree that was to come down in good time – remorseless twins they are for striding through their human forests, notching as they go – while the countenance of Son was crossed with a thousand little creases, which the same deceitful Time would take delight in smoothing out and wearing away with the flat part of his scythe, as a preparation of the surface for his deeper operations.

Dombey, exulting in the long-looked-for event, jingled and jingled the heavy gold watch-chain that depended from below his trim blue coat, whereof the buttons sparkled phosphorescently in the feeble rays of the distant fire. Son, with his little fists curled up and clenched, seemed, in his feeble way, to be squaring at existence for having come upon him so unexpectedly.

from *Dombey and Son*, Charles Dickens (1812–70)

When I was Christened

When I was christened
they held me up
and poured some water
out of a cup.

The trouble was
it fell on me,
and I and water
don't agree.

A lot of christeners
stood and listened:
I let them know
that I was christened.

David McCord
(1897–1997)

'What shall the baby be called?'

The afternoon being wet we gathered round the billiard-room fire and went into committee.

'The question before the House', said Archie, 'is, what shall the baby be called, and why. Dahlia and I have practically decided on his names, but it would amuse us to hear your inferior suggestions and point out how ridiculous they are.'

Godfather Simpson looked across in amazement at Godfather Thomas.

'Really, you are taking a good deal upon yourself, Archie,' he said coldly. 'It is entirely a matter for my colleague and myself to decide whether the ground is fit for – to decide, I should say, what the child is to be called. Unless this is quite understood we shall hand in our resignations.'

'We've been giving a lot of thought to it,' said Thomas, opening his eyes for a moment. 'And our time is valuable.' He arranged the cushions at his back and closed his eyes again.

'Well, as a matter of fact, the competition isn't quite closed,' said Archie. 'Entries can still be received.'

'We haven't really decided at all,' put in Dahlia gently. 'It is so difficult.'

'In that case,' said Samuel, 'Thomas and I will continue to act. It is my pleasant duty to inform you that we had a long consultation yesterday, and finally agreed to call him – er – Samuel Thomas.'

'Thomas Samuel,' said Thomas sleepily.

'How did you think of those names?' I asked. 'It must have taken you a tremendous time.'

'With a name like Samuel Thomas Mannering', went on Simpson ['Thomas Samuel Mannering,' murmured Thomas], 'your child might achieve almost anything. In private life you would probably call him Sam.'

'Tom,' said a tired voice.

'Or, more, familiarly, Sammy.'

'Tommy,' came in a whisper from the sofa.

'What do you think of it?' asked Dahlia.

'I mustn't say,' said Archie; 'they're my guests. But I'll tell you privately some time.'

There was silence for a little, and then a thought occurred to me.

'You know, Archie,' I said, 'limited as their ideas are, you're rather in their power. Because I was looking through the service in church on Sunday, and there comes a point when the clergyman says to the godfathers, "Name this child." Well, there you are, you know. They've got you. You may have fixed on Montmorency Plantagenet, but they've only to say "Bert", and the thing is done.'

from *The Heir*, A. A. Milne (1882–1956)

If you can keep your head when all about you . . .

Giving birth and nourishing,
having without possessing,
acting with no expectations,
leading and not trying to control:
this is the supreme virtue.

Tao Te Ching

If –

If you can keep your head when all about you
    Are losing theirs and blaming it on you,
If you can trust yourself when all men doubt you,
    But make allowance for their doubting too;
If you can wait and not be tired by waiting,
    Or being lied about, don't deal in lies,
Or being hated don't give way to hating,
    And yet don't look too good, nor talk too wise:

If you can dream – and not make dreams your master;
    If you can think – and not make thoughts your aim:
If you can meet with Triumph and Disaster
    And treat those two impostors just the same;
If you can bear to hear the truth you've spoken
    Twisted by knaves to make a trap for fools.
Or watch the things you gave your life to, broken,
    And stoop and build 'em up with worn-out tools;

If you can make one heap of all your winnings
    And risk it on one turn of pitch-and-toss,
And lose, and start again at your beginnings
    And never breathe a word about your loss;
If you can force your heart and nerve and sinew
    To serve your turn long after they are gone,
And so hold on when there is nothing in you
    Except the Will which says to them: 'Hold on!'

If you can talk with crowds and keep your virtue.
    Or walk with Kings – nor lose the common touch,
If neither foes nor loving friends can hurt you,
    If all men count with you, but none too much:
If you can fill the unforgiving minute
    With sixty seconds' worth of distance run,
Yours is the Earth and everything that's in it,
    And – which is more – you'll be a Man, my son!

Rudyard Kipling (1865–1936)

'As kingfishers catch fire, dragonflies draw flame'

As kingfishers catch fire, dragonflies draw flame;
As tumbled over rim in roundy wells
Stones ring; like each tucked string tells, each hung bell's
Bow swung finds tongue to fling out broad its name;
Each mortal thing does one thing and the same:
Deals out that being indoors each one dwells;
Selves – goes itself; *myself* it speaks and spells,
Crying *What I do is me: for that I came.*

I say more: the just man justices;
Kéeps gráce: thát keeps all his goings graces;
Acts in God's eye what in God's eye he is –
Christ – for Christ plays in ten thousand places,
Lovely in limbs, and lovely in eyes not his
To the Father through the features of men's faces.

Gerard Manley Hopkins (1844–89)

'Into your midst has come a new life'

Sun, Moon, Stars, all you that move in the heavens, hear us!
Into your midst has come a new life.
Make his path smooth that he may reach the brow of the first
hill!

Winds, Clouds, Rain, Mist, all you that move in the air, hear us!
Into your midst has come a new life.
Make his path smooth that he may reach the brow of the
second hill!

Hills, Valleys, Rivers, Lakes, Trees, grasses, all you of the earth,
hear us!
Into your midst has come a new life.
Make his path smooth that he may reach the brow of the third
hill!

Birds, great and small, that fly in the air,
Animals, great and small, that dwell in the forest,
Insects that creep among the grasses and burrow in the ground,
hear us!
Into your midst has come a new life.
Make his path smooth that he may reach the brow of the
fourth hill!

All you of the heavens, all you of the air, all you of the earth,
hear us!
Into your midst has come a new life.
Make his path smooth, then he shall travel beyond the four
hills!

Omaha Native American

Wishes for a Little Girl

What would I ask the kindly fates to give
   To crown her life, if I could have my way?
My strongest wishes would be negative,
   If they would but obey.

Give her not greatness. For great souls must stand
   Alone and lonely in this little world;
Cleft rocks that show the great Creator's hand,
   Thither by earthquakes hurled.

Give her not genius. Spare her the cruel pain
   Of finding her whole life a prey for daws;
Of bearing with quickened sense and burning brain
   The world's sneer-tinged applause.

Give her not perfect beauty's gifts. For then
   Her truthful mirror would infuse her mind
With love for self, and for the praise of men,
   That lowers woman-kind.

But make her fair and comely to the sight,
   Give her more heart than brain, more love than pride,
Let her be tender-thoughted, cheerful, bright,
   Some strong man's star and guide.

Not vainly questioning why she was sent
   Into this restless world of toil and strife,
Let her go bravely on her way, content
   To make the best of life.

Ella Wheeler Wilcox (1855–1919)

To the Newborn

May the deer make a path for you
May the eagle circle you three times
May the hare teach you tricks
And the snake go always before you

May the horse stir the wind for you
May the dove sing sweetly to you
May the dog go always beside you
And the wolf sit at your feet

May the heron be your sentinel
May the lynx stand fast at your door
May the raven bring rain to cool you
And the hummingbird bring sunlight

May you lie in the eye of the tiger
May the toad deliver its jewel to you
May the wren weave its spell for you
And the fox be your teller of tales

May you walk in grasslands and in snow
With love at your side

Traditional,
adapted by Claire Beddowes (1953–)

Born Yesterday

Tightly-folded bud,
I have wished you something
None of the others would:
Not the usual stuff
About being beautiful,
Or running off a spring
Of innocence and love –
They will all wish you that,
And should it prove possible,
Well, you're a lucky girl.

But if it shouldn't, then
May you be ordinary;
Have, like other women,
An average of talents:
Not ugly, not good-looking,
Nothing uncustomary
To pull you off your balance,
That, unworkable itself,
Stops all the rest from working.
In fact, may you be dull –
If that is what a skilled,
Vigilant, flexible,
Unemphasized, enthralled
Catching of happiness is called.

Philip Larkin (1922–85)

Forever Young

May God bless and keep you always,
May your wishes all come true,
May you always do for others
And let others do for you.
May you build a ladder to the stars
And climb on every rung,
May you stay forever young,
Forever young, forever young,
May you stay forever young.

May you grow up to be righteous,
May you grow up to be true,
May you always know the truth
And see the lights surrounding you.
May you always be courageous,
Stand upright and be strong,
May you stay forever young,
Forever young, forever young,
May you stay forever young.

May your hands always be busy,
May your feet always be swift,
May you have a strong foundation
When the winds of changes shift.
May your heart always be joyful,
May your song always be sung,
May you stay forever young,
Forever young, forever young,
May you stay forever young.

Bob Dylan (1941–)

'Speak to us of Children'

And a woman who held a babe against her bosom said, Speak
to us of Children.
And he said:
Your children are not your children.
They are the sons and daughters of Life's longing for itself.
They come through you but not from you,
And though they are with you yet they belong not to you.

You may give them your love but not your thoughts,
For they have their own thoughts.
You may house their bodies but not their souls,
For their souls dwell in the house of to-morrow, which you
cannot visit, not even in your dreams.

You may strive to be like them, but seek not to make them
like you.
For life goes not backward nor tarries with yesterday.
You are the bows from which your children as living arrows
are sent forth.
The archer sees the mark upon the path of the infinite, and
He bends you with His might that His arrows may go swift
and far.
Let your bending in the Archer's hand be for gladness;
For even as He loves the arrow that flies, so He loves also
the bow that is stable.

from *The Prophet*, Kalil Gibran (1883–1931)

But One

Life is no rehearsal
   Life is what it is
Today is the only time
   That today is.

Life is full of change
   A mountain to be climbed
An opportunity to explore
   Its drifting sands combined.

Life can be a challenge
   To be grasped with both hands
Acknowledging the journey
   Open-eyed yet unplanned.

Life can be sad or uncertain
   And fill us with great fear
But always it is precious
   Its winding path unclear.

Life can be so peaceful
   In the early hours of dawn
Or take on all the ravages of time
   And make us feel forlorn.

Life is no rehearsal
   Life is what it is
Today is the only time
   That today is.

Gloria Hargreaves

'But now this is the word of the Lord'

But now this is the word of the Lord,
the word of your creator, O Jacob,
of him who fashioned you, Israel:

Have no fear; for I have paid your ransom;
I have called you by name and you are my own.
When you pass through deep waters, I am with you,
when you pass through rivers,
they will not sweep you away;
walk through fire and you will not be scorched,
through flames and they will not burn you.
For I am the Lord your God,
the Holy One of Israel, your deliverer.

Bring my sons and daughters from afar,
bring them from the ends of the earth;
bring every one who is called by my name,
all whom I have created, whom I have formed,
all whom I have made for my glory.

Isaiah 43:1–3, 6–7 (New English Bible)

'I know what life is'

I have seen a mother at a cot . . . so I know what love is'

I have looked into the eyes of a child . . . so I know what faith is;

I have seen a rainbow . . . so I know what beauty is;

I have felt the pounding of the sea . . . so I know what power is;

I have planted a tree . . . so I know what hope is;

I have heard a wild bird sing . . . so I know what freedom is;

I have seen a chrysalis burst into life . . . so I know what mystery is;

I have lost a friend . . . so I know what sorrow is;

I have seen a star-decked sky . . . so I know what infinity is;

I have seen and felt all these things . . . so I know what life is.

Anonymous

'Children have rights'

Children have rights:

The right to equality, regardless of race, colour, religion, sex and nationality

The right to healthy mental and physical development

The right to a name and nationality

The right to sufficient food, housing and medical care

The right to special care if handicapped

The right to love, understanding and care

The right to free education, play and recreation

The right to immediate aid in the event of disasters and emergencies

The right to protection from cruelty, neglect and exploitation

The right to protection from persecution and to an upbringing of the spirit of (sisterhood), brotherhood and peace.

from 'Declaration of the Rights of the Child',
adopted unanimously on 20 November 1959 by the General Assembly of the United Nations

Give a Little

Give a little
Take a little
Is what we learn through life
It doesn't always work this way
We often say that's life
You always have the givers
Constantly they seem
To help whoever comes their way
And give their love and dreams
Then you have the takers
Through life this does ring true
They always grab what they are given
Give nothing in return
But try and be a giver
You will reap such rich rewards
Believe me who comes knocking
It's love there at your door

Jeanette Gaffney

'Whatsoever things are true'

Whatsoever things are true,
whatsoever things are honest,
whatsoever things are just,
whatsoever things are pure,
whatsoever things are lovely,
whatsoever things are of good report:
if there be any virtue,
and if there be any praise,
think on these things.

Philippians 4:8 (King James version)

The Character of a Happy Life

How happy is he born and taught
That serveth not another's will;
Whose armour is his honest thought,
And simple truth his utmost skill!

Whose passions not his masters are;
Whose soul is still prepared for death,
Untied unto the world by care
Of public fame or private breath;

Who envies none that chance doth raise,
Nor vice; who never understood
How deepest wounds are given by praise;
Nor rules of state, but rules of good;

Who hath his life from rumours freed;
Whose conscience is his strong retreat;
Whose state can neither flatterers feed,
Nor ruin make oppressors great;

Who God doth late and early pray
More of His grace than gifts to lend;
And entertains the harmless day
With a religious book or friend;

– This man is freed from servile bands
Of hope to rise or fear to fall:
Lord of himself, though not of lands,
And having nothing, yet hath all.

Sir Henry Wotton (1568–1639)

'Now this is the day'

Now this is the day.
Our child,
Into the daylight
You will go out standing.
Preparing for your day.

Our child, it is your day,
This day.
May your road be fulfilled.
In your thoughts may we live,
May we be the ones whom your thoughts will embrace,
May you help us all to finish our roads.

Zuni Indian

Expect Nothing

Expect nothing. Live frugally
on surprise.
Become a stranger
To need of pity
Or, if compassion be freely
Given out
Take only enough
Stop short of urge to plead
Then purge away the need.

Wish for nothing larger
Than your own small heart
Or greater than a star;
Tame wild disappointment
With caress
Unmoved and cold
Make of it a parka
For your soul.

Discover the reason why
So tiny human giant
Exists at all.
So scared unwise
But expect nothing. Live frugally
on surprise.

Alice Walker (1944–)

Progress

Let there be many windows to your soul,
That all the glory of the universe
May beautify it. Not the narrow pane
Of one poor creed can catch the radiant rays
That shine from countless sources. Tear away
The blinds of superstition; let the light
Pour through fair windows broad as Truth itself
And high as God.
                    Why should the spirit peer
Through some priest-curtained orifice, and grope
Along dim corridors of doubt, when all
The splendour from unfathomed seas of space
Might bathe it with the golden waves of Love?
Sweep up the debris of decaying faiths;
Sweep down the cobwebs of worn-out beliefs,
And throw your soul wide open to the light
Of Reason and of Knowledge. Tune your ear
To all the wordless music of the stars
And to the voice of Nature, and your heart
Shall turn to truth and goodness, as the plant
Turns to the sun. A thousand unseen hands
Reach down to help you to their peace-crowned heights,
And all the forces of the firmament
Shall fortify your strength. Be not afraid
To thrust aside half-truths and grasp the whole.

Ella Wheeler Wilcox (1855–1919)

Birth Baptism

The little drop of the Father
On thy little forehead, beloved one.

The little drop of the Son
On thy little forehead, beloved one.

The little drop of the Spirit
On thy little forehead beloved one.

To aid thee from the fays,
To guard thee from the host;

To aid thee from the gnome,
To shield thee from the spectre;

To keep thee for the Three,
To shield thee, to surround thee;

To save thee for the Three,
To fill thee with the graces;

The little drop of the Three
To lave thee with the graces.

Anonymous

Show Me the Way

Show me the way that leads to the true life,
   I do not care what tempests may assail me,
I shall be given courage for the strife,
   I know my strength will not desert or fail me;
I know that I shall conquer in the fray:
               Show me the way.

Show me the way up to a higher plane,
   Where body shall be servant to the soul.
I do not care what tides of woe, or pain,
   Across my life their angry waves may roll
If I but reach the end I seek some day:
               Show me the way.

Show me the way, and let me bravely climb
   Above vain grievings for unworthy treasures;
Above all sorrow that finds balm in time –
   Above small triumphs, or belittling pleasures;
Up to those heights where these things seem child's play:
               Show me the way.

Show me the way to that calm, perfect peace
   Which springs from an inward consciousness of right;
To where all conflicts with the flesh shall cease,
   And self shall radiate with the spirit's light.
Though hard the journey and the strife, I pray
               Show me the way.

Ella Wheeler Wilcox (1855–1919)

The Rainbow

My heart leaps up when I behold
A rainbow in the sky:
So was it when my life began;
So is it now I am a man;
So be it when I shall grow old,
        Or let me die!
The Child is father of the Man;
And I could wish my days to be
Bound each to each by natural piety.

William Wordsworth (1770–1850)

'I know this'

I know this . . .
I know not if the voice of a man can reach the sky;
I know not if the mighty one will hear as I pray;
I know not if the gifts I ask will be granted;
I know not if we can truly hear the world of old;
I know not what will come to pass in our future days;
I only hope that good will come, my child, to you.

The Gabrielinos

Four Things

Four things a man must learn to do
If he would make his record true:
To think without confusion clearly:
To love his fellow-men sincerely:
To act from honest motives purely:
To trust in God and Heaven securely.

Henry Van Dyke (1852–1933)

'Let the children come to me'

They brought children for him to touch; and the disciples scolded them for it. But when Jesus saw this he was indignant, and said to them, 'Let the children come to me; do not try to stop them; for the kingdom of God belongs to such as these. I tell you, whoever does not accept the kingdom of God like a child will never enter it.' And he put his arms round them, laid his hands upon them, and blessed them.

As he was starting out on a journey, a stranger ran up, and, kneeling before him, asked, 'Good Master, what must I do to win eternal life?' Jesus said to him, 'Why do you call me good? No one is good except God alone. You know the commandments: "Do not murder; do not commit adultery; do not steal; do not give false evidence; do not defraud; honour your father and mother."'

Mark 10:13–19 (New English Bible)

What is Good

'What is the real good?'
I asked in musing mood.

Order, said the law court;
Knowledge, said the school;
Truth, said the wise man;
Pleasure, said the fool;
Love, said the maiden;
Beauty, said the page;
Freedom, said the dreamer;
Home, said the sage;
Fame, said the soldier;
Equity, the seer:
Spake my heart full sadly,
'The answer is not here.'

Then within my bosom
Softly this I heard:
'Each heart holds the secret;
Kindness is the word.'

John Boyle O'Reilly (1844–90)

The Naming Ceremony

The naming ceremony below has been written specially for this book. A common name has been chosen for the child as well as for the sponsors; it seemed preferable to leaving blanks. By the same token, the ceremony has been written for a girl in order to avoid having to write 'his/hers' (or even 'theirs'). It's clear how the ceremony can be adapted as needed. Obviously, this will be modified according to the preferences of those involved.

The usual name for the person leading the ceremony is the 'celebrant', and it seemed useful to leave that unchanged. If the ceremony is not being led by a professional or taking place under the aegis of local government, the celebrant can be anyone: a parent, a grandparent, a family friend, one of the sponsors (sometimes called mentors or supporters), even an elder sibling, perhaps. The sponsors are, of course, filling the roles that would usually be given to godparents at a christening. Choose your sponsors with care. They should be people who will live up to the promises they will make at the ceremony. They should also be people the child will see often as she is growing up.

Naming ceremonies can be held anywhere. Official ones will be held at the register office or at some similar venue that 'conforms to health and safety regulations'. Official ceremonies have to be paid for (rates available from your local council office). You will also receive a 'souvenir record certificate' of the event.

If you choose to hold your own ceremony, you can have it pretty much anywhere: your house, your garden, on a beach, in a stone circle (check where permission might be required). You can add music, especially if you have friends who are musically talented: what better than to greet the child with a piece of live music or song? Candles can be lit and held, incense burned, a tree planted, the child's astrological birth chart displayed or read out – whatever pleases those taking part.

Your own souvenir of the event might be a book in which everyone present writes a few words. Later, photographs of the ceremony could be added to the book, along with copies of the poems or readings and an account of the day written by one of those present. A flower, picked on that day, might be pressed between the pages . . . There are many possibilities. The parents or the sponsors or the grandparents, of all these together, might wish to endow the child with a gift: something that the child can keep always, a token.

The readings can be given by anyone present. The parents and sponsors will have specific roles to play in the ceremony, though one or another of them might also want to read. If not, the role could be given to a grandparent, an elder brother or sister, or a close friend of the family. Similarly, the order of speaking during the naming ceremony can be reversed; maybe the mother speaks first if the child is a girl, the father if it's a boy.

All these decisions are personal; nothing's fixed. The ceremony given below is an example, a guide. Much can be added. For instance, the parents might like to say why they chose the name: perhaps there's a family tradition involved or the name was chosen for its particular meaning.

Finally, think of involving at the outset all those playing a principal role – sponsors, grandparents, close friends – to create a naming ceremony that will please all of you. Adapt the ceremony to your purpose; ensure no one is uncomfortable with the promises they are asked to make or the passages they are asked to read; think about the special talents of some of those involved and what they might contribute; if there are other children in the family, give them a role to play (they might like to design the invitations, for example); and, as always, make sure people speak up when they read.

A Naming Ceremony

THE WELCOME

CELEBRANT: We are here today to name this child and to welcome her to the world. At the beginning of this new life, we reach out to greet and protect her, to love and to hold her, to draw her towards the circle of family and friends that will care for her and watch her grow. Everyone here has a special relationship with this child – we affirm that simply by being here. She is already a part of our lives. Now her name will be added to those names we love; names that are part of our everyday living. This name is hers to own and ours to celebrate.

READING

A poem or a piece of prose read by a friend or relative.

THE NAMING

(Celebrant, parents and sponsors)

CELEBRANT: The given names of this child are Mary Jane.

MOTHER: This is my daughter, Mary Jane.

FATHER: This is Mary Jane, my daughter.

CELEBRANT: You have given life to Mary Jane and brought her into the world. Will you care for her, protect her and guide her?

MOTHER AND FATHER: Yes, we will.

CELEBRANT: Will you do all that you can to keep her from harm?

MOTHER AND FATHER: Yes, we will.

CELEBRANT: Will you help her to value those qualities that bring kindness, tolerance and respect for others?

MOTHER AND FATHER: Yes, we will.

CELEBRANT: Will you have the courage to let her go when she is ready to make her own way in the world?

MOTHER AND FATHER: Yes, we will.

The celebrant calls forward the sponsors by name.

CELEBRANT: Mary Jane's sponsors are George and Katherine.

George and Katherine step forward.

THE SPONSORS' PROMISES

(Celebrant and sponsors)

CELEBRANT: Katherine, you have chosen to be one of those who will give Mary help and encouragement as she is growing up. Do you promise to be her guide and her friend? Do you promise to give support to her and her parents when it's needed? Do you promise always to look upon her with fondness and consider her a special person in your life?

KATHERINE: I promise.

CELEBRANT: George, you have chosen to be one of those who will give Mary help and encouragement as she is growing up. Do you promise to be her guide and her friend? Do you promise to give support to her and her parents when it's needed? Do you promise always to look upon her with fondness and consider her a special person in your life?

GEORGE: I promise.

If the sponsors have brought a gift for the child, they should now hand it to the celebrant or to the mother. If this is the case, the following words might be spoken:

KATHERINE: I give this as a token of my promise to Mary Jane.

GEORGE: I give this as a token of my promise to Mary Jane.

READING

(*Again, by a friend or relative*)

> *After the reading, music might be played. When this is over, the celebrant lights a candle.*

CELEBRANT: Each new life brings hope to the world. I light this candle to mark the naming of Mary Jane Smith.

> *The parents step forward and share the final reading, the poem 'Pledge' by Dora Mann:*

FINAL READING

MOTHER: Here in my cradling arms
           Safe from any harm
           Let the loved-one lie.

FATHER: There's room for you in my heart
           And room for you in my house
           Until the day I die.

CELEBRANT: Welcome, Mary Jane.
ALL PRESENT: Welcome, Mary Jane.

Notes

p. 73 'Waking with Russell': *mezzo del cammin* means 'the middle of the road', as in the opening lines of Dante's *Inferno*: 'Nel mezzo del cammin di nostra vita' ('In the middle of the road of our life').

p. 74 'Once more the storm is howling': The setting for this poem is Yeats's home Thoor Ballylee, near Lady Gregory's estate, Coole Park. Lady Gregory, playwright, theatre director and folklorist, was Yeats's longtime friend and sometime collaborator.

p. 91 'The End': Christopher Robin Milne was the son of A. A. Milne and the model for Christopher Robin.

p. 100 'Who do you think he is like?': *nem.con.*: *nemine contradicente*, with no one dissenting, unanimously.

p. 125 'Now this is the day': The Zuni Indians were indigenous to New Mexico. The Zuni reservation was built in 1695 on the site of the seven original villages attacked by Coronado in 1540. They were best known for their ceremonial dances.

p. 131 'I know this': The Gabrielinos lived on the islands and mainland of the Los Angeles Basin and its surrounding valleys, and survived by hunting and fishing. It is known that this area has been inhabited for at least 10,000 years.

Acknowledgements

JAMES BERRY: 'Isn't My Name Magical?' from *Isn't My Name Magical?* (copyright © James Berry, 1991) is reproduced by permission of PFD (www.pfd.co.uk) on behalf of James Berry

JENI COUZYN: 'Creation' from *A Time to be Born: Poems of Childbirth* (Fire Lizard). Reproduced by permission of Jeni Couzyn

BRUCE DAWE: 'Condolences of the Season' from *Sometimes Gladness* (Pearson Australia, fifth edition). Reproduced by permission of Pearson Education Australia

MARGARET DRABBLE: Extract from *The Millstone* (Weidenfeld & Nicolson). Reproduced by permission of Weidenfeld & Nicolson, a division of the Orion Publishing Group, as the publisher

VICKI FEAVER: 'Children' from *Relative Values* by Vicki Feaver (Secker & Warburg). Reproduced by permission of Vicki Feaver

JOHN FULLER: 'Birth Bells for Louisa' from *Now and for a Time* by John Fuller published by Chatto & Windus. Reprinted by permission of the Random House Group

DESMOND GRAHAM: 'Like a fish out of God's hand'. Reproduced by permission of the Flambard Press from *Milena Poems* (2004)

THOM GUNN: 'Baby Song' from *Jack Straw's Castle* by Thom Gunn (Faber and Faber). Reproduced by permission of Faber and Faber

GLORIA HARGREAVES: 'But One' from *A Glimpse at Life* (Poetry Today, an imprint of Penhaligon Page Ltd). Reproduced by permission of Gloria Hargreaves

BOB KAUFMAN: 'Response (for Eileen)' from *Solitudes Crowded with Loneliness*, copyright © 1965 by Bob Kaufman. Reprinted by permission of New Directions Publishing Corp.

RUDYARD KIPLING: 'If –' reprinted by permission of A. P. Watt Ltd on behalf of the National Trust for Places of Historical Interest or Natural Beauty

142